MW00952350

This Journal Belongs to:

....

Made in the USA
Las Vegas, NV
21 February 2023

67912235R00069